for Thomas,
who made them fun—M.D.

* * *

for Jen,
my honey bunny—D.S.

Book design by Kristen M. Nobles.

Typeset in Retrofit and Coop Light.

The illustrations in this book were hand drawn and then digitally reworked using Macromedia FreeHand and Adobe Photoshop software.

Manufactured in China.

Library of Congress Cataloging-in-Publication Data
Downs, Mike.
Pig giggles and rabbit rhymes / by Mike Downs ; illustrated by David Sheldon.
  p. cm.
  Summary: Presents more than twenty simple animal jokes.
  ISBN 0-8118-3114-0
  1. Riddles, Juvenile. 2. Animals-Juvenile humor. [1. Riddles. 2.
Jokes. 3. Animals-Humor.]   1. Sheldon, David, 1957-   . ill. II. Title.
PN6371.5 .D68 2002
398.6-dc21
2001003885

Distributed in Canada by Raincoast Books
9050 Shaughnessy Street, Vancouver, British Columbia V6P 6E5

10 9 8 7 6 5 4 3 2 1

Chronicle Books LLC
85 Second Street, San Francisco, California 94105
www.chroniclekids.com

Pig Giggles and Rabbit Rhymes

A Book of Animal Riddles

What rhymes with dog?

By Mike Downs * Illustrated by David Sheldon

chronicle books

What is an **eight-legged creature's** favorite **drink**?

Le Menu

What is a **frog's** favorite **dessert**?

Spider cider

 Fly pie

What does an OCTOPUS like to SiP?

What was the CruStacean musical group called?

Ink drink

Sand band

Raccoon spoon

Quill
grill

What does a **billy** go **sailing** in?

What kind of **story** did the **orca** tell?

Goat
boat

Whale
tale

What do sly
mammals
wear on
their feet?

shoes

What does a hog wear
if she wants some hair?

Fox socks

Pig
wig

Duck truck

Mule tool

What do **joeys** use to **wash** their hair?

What do **hooting birds** use to **dry** off?

Kangaroo shampoo

Owl towel

Alligator elevator

Jolly Polly

Polite termite

TO: Bug

Dear Bug
Thank You!
Dinner was delicious.
Your friend,
Termite

Bug rug

What do you call a **rabbit** that tells **jokes?**

What does a **grizzly** sit on?

funny bunny

 Bear chair